ENSURING BUSINESS GROWTH: How to lead a successful business.

Donald Watkins

Chapter One

Things That Are Sold

The range of goods that individuals purchase and sell on the streets is expanding. Finding the greatest items for your consumers and the best business plan for you is your duty.

I've put up a list of product categories that can help your company expand rapidly. Simply continue with the book if these items don't fit you or if you already know what you want to offer. If not, it's essential to carefully look over each product to pick the one that would catch your attention.

1. t-shirts

Nothing else dares to dethrone this king of personalized apparel. There is a wide range of sizes and colours available for t-shirts. Selecting the incorrect shirt is almost impossible, although it may appear hard to choose from the many shirt kinds.

Pro tip: Choose cosy clothing and indicate which printing technique you want. The most crucial factor is the print quality.

2. Decorative Arts and Additional Digital Items

Decorative Arts and Additional Digital Items
Art belongs beyond small-town artisan fairs. Buying or selling anything doesn't even need you to leave your home. You could want to offer digital printouts of your artwork, stock images, or even music.

You may also sell hard versions of your digital artwork as posters, canvases, mugs, and other items via Print on Demand.

Pro tip: To find out how your favourite artists are generating income from their talents, check in with them and the community.

3. Magnets and Stickers

Every laptop may be used as a sticker sheet, and every fridge should have at least one if not many, magnets. The key takeaway from this is that consumers like these products and purchase them often and in huge amounts. At local markets or via your internet shop, stickers and magnets may be a reliable source of additional revenue.

Pro tip: Since there is a large consumer overlap, offer both stickers and magnets in your business.

4. Beauty & Cosmetics Items
Beauty & Cosmetics Items
Beauty and cosmetic items are in high demand since so many people use them and use them quickly. You'd better remember that the hottest trend of the century for your product line is natural cosmetics.
Keep in mind that makeup requires room for storage, thus makeup bags fall under this product category.

Pro tip: Keep in mind that not everyone has the same appearance. Provide a range that suits different skin types if you want to increase your clientele.

5. Wall Décor

It is essentially a blank canvas on which you create and market your ideas, therefore it is constantly current and innovative. Posters, both framed and unframed, and canvases that you can display on any wall in your home are popular items in this category. Some are designed to be put outside as well.

Pro tip: To encourage your consumers to buy more than one artwork, put together a themed collection of related prints.

6. Present Baskets

Present Baskets

While it's rare for someone to have the time in today's hectic world to put together a meaningful gift basket for friends and family, everyone enjoys receiving and giving gift baskets. Gift baskets may include any assortment of goods, from collectables to perishables.

Pro tip: Since you'll be presenting the whole package as a purchasable commodity, give the contents and the gift basket itself equal consideration.

7. Marketing Virtual Courses

The popularity of DIY projects and learning new crafts online has increased lately. Selling online is as simple as it sounds: identify your strengths, take more courses to hone your abilities, and then capitalize on your connections.

Sell online courses to supplement your revenue, even if it's not your primary source of money.

Expert advice: Ensure that your webcam has a high-quality microphone. A decent smartphone is another option.

8. Accessories and Cases for Phones

Since most individuals carry a phone about all the time, phone covers and other phone accessories are a profitable product area to produce and market. There are many varieties of phone cases, including flip cases, transparent, durable, biodegradable, and soft cases.

Pro tip: Expand your collection of phone case models to attract more customers.

9. Subscription Cases
Subscription Box
Well-curated product boxes are among the newest and most popular items in the eCommerce space. A box of gourmet cheeses, a box of toys and treats for dogs, or even a box of books might be the contents. You may create subscription boxes based on every one of your customers' interests.

Expert advice: Each month, use the same size package. To ensure that your clients find value in your subscription boxes and that it doesn't become out of control, think about focusing your company on consumables or collectables.

10. Supplies for Pets
Pet owners are always searching for supplies for their reptiles and furry companions. You may start your own craft company by making and selling handmade dog treats or felt ball bags.

The ideal toys and treats will mostly rely on the dogs and pet owners you cater to.

Pro tip: Since dogs are just as finicky as their owners, provide a range of tastes and toy varieties.

11. Bath Bombs

An iconic item that is always in trend is the bath bomb. Naturally, this is only applicable to those who own bathtubs in which to use bath bombs. They are fantastic for children, adults, and yes, even dogs. They come in a variety of entertaining forms, colours, smells, and foam kinds.

Pro tip: If a client doesn't enjoy bath bombs or doesn't have a bathtub at home, offer them alternatives that are just as interesting.

12. Pottery

Pottery

Ceramic products have a certain quality to them and are practically required for every firm that sells crafts. You may create and market clay bracelets, earrings, mugs, plates, and vases. Join us in reintroducing porcelain figurines to the general public as a way to add flair to any interior design.

Pro tip: A lot of POD websites provide personalized ceramic items as
Mugs and holiday decorations.

13. Jewels

Handmade goods are in high demand, but POD services may also be used to create and market jewellery, which can include everything from elegant engravings to vibrant graphics. Jewellery is available in a variety of materials and styles.

Pro tip: Consider giving items of jewellery that may be customized. Regardless of
People will be searching for customized presents that allow them to add a name, such as necklaces or pet tags.

14. Socks

Even though a sock company may not seem like a good concept at first, it is a feasible business venture. The first layer of comfortable cloth on your feet is socks. There are also many different sizes and forms for socks.

Expert advice: Don't be scared to adorn socks with your wildest and brightest patterns. People have an about equal fondness for socks and colours.

15. Throws

Throughout the year, blankets are a terrific product to manufacture and sell online since they are essential on chilly winter evenings and make for delightful summer days. They provide really beautiful all-over designs and are fluffy and silky.

Expert advice: Avoid using minute details in your blanket designs since the print will seem hazy.

16. Pins made of enamel

Adoration for enamel pins is almost as widespread as that of stickers. You can create almost any design for people to wear on their clothes and bags, which makes it a genuinely unique product to develop and sell.

Pro tip: Create themed sets to encourage multiple orders from your clients.

17. Essential oils and candles
Essential oils and candles
Create and promote candles, t-shirts, and bath bombs at neighbourhood fairs or from the comfort of your own home via internet markets. Essential oils remain a specialist craft, ideal for your do-it-yourself company and craft fairs.

Pro tip: To serve a much wider clientele, provide a variety of smells.

18. Kitchenware Accessory
Kitchen accessories are always in high demand since they are constantly in use, much like other perishable goods. Create and market your goods,

or use POD, which offers bento boxes, mittens, aprons, and more.

Pro tip: To determine whether handcrafted goods or customisable products might sell well online, see what your target clients are preparing.

19. Personalized Items
Personalized Items
Everything has a specialized market, therefore you may use your shop or seller account to produce and promote your artistic products. Your store can become the destination for unique presents and other handcrafted goods.

Pro tip: Start an Etsy store or something similar. People go there to discover one-of-a-kind, handcrafted, and vintage goods.
..20. Tote Bags
Wearable art may be found in totes. Some claim that since they fold up small enough to fit in your pocket and are large enough to accommodate all of your groceries on the way home, they are more useful than digital

downloads. They are also excellent as surfaces for enamel pins.

Expert advice: Create totes that complement other items of apparel you're selling.

Chapter Two

Choosing the Market to Target

After deciding on your company's goods and services, you need to decide who your target customer base is. The real consumer base, or audience, that your company will try to sell its goods and services to is known as the target market. Even though you cannot possibly reach every member of your target market, focusing your services on that segment can greatly facilitate sales.

1.

Examine the characteristics of your offerings. Ascertain the advantages that your items provide for your clients and how they meet their demands. To facilitate the analysis, enumerate such characteristics and requirements.

2.

Examine the kinds of clients who are most likely to buy from you and use your services. Take into account factors like age, gender, marital status, income, employment, educational attainment, and ethnic background. Determine which consumer segments need your items the most.

3.

Take into account the individual traits of your possible clients and ascertain how their lifestyle influences the needs of your offerings. Consider the customer's values, interests, and character attributes. Think of the qualities that will appeal to your consumers as well as how and when they will utilize your services.

4.

Examine who your competitors' target customers are. Examine the requirements that your rivals meet for their intended clientele. Determine which segments of the market the competition has ignored. Instead of going for the same market as your rivals, try to close the gap in the market.

5.

If your company is up and running, have a look at your present clientele. Determine which goods or services appeal to your present clientele and what advantages they get from using them.

6.

Gather the results of all your studies. Determine which consumer categories are most in need of your services based on your results. To ensure that your target market is neither too large nor too tiny, keep the market well-balanced.

You may boost income by focusing on the requirements and wants of your customers.
Increasing output and service quality is one of every company's main objectives as it will boost sales. Businesses must continually adapt to the changing demands of their consumers and the times to achieve this effectively. Knowing what your clients want will enable you to change and advance with the times. Customer requirements also evolve with the times. Your company has to be adaptable and keep an eye on the calibre of its offerings.

Emphasis on the Customer

Companies may use a range of techniques to ascertain the services, commodities, or products that their present or potential clients are interested in. A customer-focused firm is committed to providing these services that are relevant and helpful to customers. Surveys and questionnaires to the target market or demography that your future product will appeal to may be needed for this study.

Client Requirements

The firm is driven by the demands of its customers. Many times, a company is founded because someone sees a need. It's critical to keep asking customers to make sure this emphasis is where it should be. Gaining new customers and supplying future items to existing ones need an understanding of consumer wants.

Sales and Marketing

A company may promote and sell its goods and services if it is committed to meeting the demands of its clients and is aware of those needs. Customers must believe that your product is worthwhile purchasing. A skilled salesperson may illustrate the need for a product in the life of a client by connecting the customer's demands with how the product or service will meet those needs. This will also direct how you choose to promote your goods and services.

Rival Services

Consider how customers are already meeting their needs for the product or service you want to provide. Take into account what your rivals provide that you do not, as well as what you have to give that they do not. This will assist you in comprehending the perspective of the customer, and you may be able to modify your offerings to better satisfy their needs.

Identify your target market to improve marketing results.

The usual client profile for your firm is your target market. To effectively and economically target your marketing, you must first identify who your target audience is. This will enable you to create content that specifically appeals to them. It is less likely to enhance sales to have a wide target audience without any particular demographics since you are not reaching the individuals who will utilize your product or service. Before starting your next marketing effort, take some time to identify the target audience.

1.

Examine the goods and services that you provide. To determine precisely who would benefit from your items, think about their features and advantages from the perspective of the user. Customers of household cleaning services, for instance, benefit from time savings; hence, the target market may include working professionals or mothers who need more time to manage work and family obligations.

2.

To assist in selecting a target audience, assess your abilities and areas of competence. A caterer with expertise in large-scale corporate events, for instance, could decide to focus on that segment of the market.

3.

Examine your existing clientele to find out who is currently making use of your offerings. Look for commonalities in your clientele's age, gender, occupation, level of education, and ethnicity. Make use of this data to focus more specifically on your target market.

4.

Find out who your rivals are promoting with their marketing. Examine the kinds of individuals who use such services and the target audiences for the marketing collateral. Determine how to search for marginally different target clients to draw in a distinct market niche. If another tutoring business, for instance, focuses on helping families with young children who need assistance with reading and arithmetic, then you should focus your service on high school students and those getting ready for standardized college admission examinations.

5.

Using the data from your study, create a basic profile of the kind of clients you want to target. Establish the ideal clientele's lifestyle, values, background, vocations, age, and region. If you provide a variety of services or goods, ascertain if a second or third target market could be interested in those particular offerings.

6.

Periodically assess your target market to see whether your offerings are still best suited for that demographic. Consider if you need to create a new profile for that core audience when you add additional goods or services.

Chapter Three

Developing Your Name

Why is having a strong brand name crucial?

A strong brand name enhances a business's identification. For example, the name of a renowned person conveys something about who they are. Before you even look at the back cover, you can tell what genre a book is even if it has "Stephen King" on it.

Brand names function similarly. Consider Apple as an example. You can tell what an Apple product will look like before you ever look at it.

Additionally, nicknames or individual names may be brands. Better known online as "Gary Vee," Gary Vaynerchuck is an internet celebrity, author, speaker, and entrepreneur. He utilizes the moniker Gary Vee to represent himself at events, on social media, and in his numerous business endeavours.

How to come up with a catchy brand name
Although there isn't a secret recipe for building a powerful brand identity, you may position yourself for success by following these guidelines:

Make it stand out.
Your brand name will stay if you use punchy, single-syllable words or rhymes that repeat sounds. Coca-Cola's clever alliteration has made it a brand that people remember. The sequence of "c" sounds facilitates memorization.

Because acronyms are short, sweet, and easy to understand, certain businesses employ them effectively. Although the American Telephone and Telegraph Company is what AT&T stands for, the former is more well-known. The "T" in AT&T is repeated, which makes it simple to say and much simpler to remember. To identify the brand, you don't need to know what the acronym means.

Make sure your spelling and pronunciation are clear.

A strong brand name must be simple to say out loud or in writing. Names that are clumsy, convoluted, or hard to pronounce are hard to remember. If you want to succeed internationally, having a simple name is very crucial since it has to sound the same in many languages and cultures.

The biggest brands are not immune to errors. Let's take another look at Coca-Cola. Coca-Cola, being one of the biggest beverage businesses globally, has a substantial marketing spend. The business changed the name to roughly translate to "mouth, happy, rejoice" — like the first taste of this drink — after realizing that "Coca-Cola" phonetically translated to "Bite the wax tadpole" when they first began marketing themselves in China in the 1920s.

Another brand name that is simple to speak and spell is Amazon. The name has three easily spoken syllables, and the Amazon River is the reason why most people are already acquainted with it. Uber employs a single, globally recognized term as both a promise and a title. Similar to how Kleenex replaced the term "facial tissue," Uber has effectively replaced the word "cab." Both are outstanding instances of branding.

arouse feelings

Strong brand names evoke strong emotions. They evoke feelings connected to the culture of the brand using effective promotion and ongoing reinforcement. People eventually develop preconceived notions or feelings in response to hearing or seeing a brand's name.

One of the biggest athletic companies in the world, for instance, is Nike. It is no secret that Nike derives its name from the Greek goddess of victory. Greek mythology and everything that it stands for—glory, grandeur, and sports—was particularly inspirational to Nike.

The brand is now closely associated with elite players commemorating victories in sports. Nike often uses athletes doing amazing achievements in its ads to uplift viewers' spirits and give them hope.

Consider a subject that is important to you and your audience. Is that a name? A location? An emblem? Use that concept to connect your brand name to feelings.

Make it ageless.
The greatest brand names are timeless, which means that they will still be relevant 20 years or 40 years from now.

Classic brand names aren't determined by fads or popular culture. If you name your business after a sentence from a popular TikTok audio, it could attract clients at first, but many people won't get the reference if the sound goes out of style.

Rather, concentrate on the message and values of your brand. Reach for thoughts that stick in your memory and human feelings like inspiration, pleasure, and hope. Recall Nike: Greek mythology and its inspirational attributes are still important in modern culture.

Let your imagination go wild online
Without writing a single line of code, create fully customized, production-ready websites or very high-fidelity prototypes. only while using Webflow.

Coming up with a brand name from the start is difficult. When brainstorming, consider the following crucial questions to ask yourself:

1. What is the essence of your brand?
What makes up your brand's "core" is its vision, goal, and philosophy. How did your brand come to be? What principles does your recently established company uphold? Establish and maintain your vision from the beginning.

Consider the components that served as inspiration for you while developing your good or service. What you provide should be reflected in your brand name. If you're launching a sports podcast, for instance, you probably want a brand name that inspires tenacity, inspiration, and motivation. As an alternative, if you're limited to only one league or sport, you may go with an onomatopoeia or pun exclusive to that league, such as "Swish" for a podcast about the WNBA.

2. What distinguishes you?
Make a list of the things your company does better than its rivals by looking at other companies in your industry. What distinguishes the brand? Your distinctive quality must be reflected in the name.

Never try to emulate someone else's success. Consider how to communicate these principles via your brand name while keeping your attention on your brand and what it has to offer.

3. Can you say something?
Remember who your target audience is at all times. Making a solid first impression is crucial

for a new brand. Think about the answers to the preceding questions and the point you want to make.

To prevent losing out on prospective clients, make sure your name aligns with your message. Different brand voices resonate with different target demographics. Consider the meditation software "Calm." Just the name of the app conveys to the user what to anticipate.

4. What marketing plan do you have?
Think about where and how you want to utilize your brand name. Is it for a shop on social media? An IT start-up? Your name should follow the path that your brand strategy establishes. Long names don't work on Instagram, and tech puns that are difficult to spell won't appear in Google searches.

In any case, take your time choosing a name. Think of a few different names, and ensure that the one you choose is both immediately usable as a domain name and legally protected.

5. Have you given it a try already?

Try it out before you register and formally commit to the name. After showing it to your loved ones, get a second assessment from strangers. Observe how they respond and get their input on how to do better. Ask folks to try reading and pronouncing it once you've written it down.

If anything you hear doesn't sit well with you, don't give up. You can always make further adjustments.

Are you feeling stuck? Utilize a brand name generator.

If you're not sure how to choose a brand name, these tools filter out names that aren't accessible and provide possibilities depending on your input using artificial intelligence (AI) and data processing.

NameSnack: NameSnack creates a variety of name styles for your company by fusing domain and keyword searches with machine learning. A logo creator is also included with this utility.

Brandroot: In only a few minutes, Brandroot, a "premium business name generator," may search the internet for names and domains that are available.

FreshBooks: Before providing you with a list of possibilities, FreshBooks poses basic inquiries about your expertise and sector.

Namelix: Namelix can design a logo with your new brand name and states that it can "generate short, brandable business names using AI."

Remember that software is impersonal and may exclude important components that you would want to include. But, if you're stuck, these tools could serve as an inspiration.

Continue developing your brand.

Developing a brand requires trial and error, particularly for newcomers. The first step to giving your business a unified identity is developing your brand name. The next step after deciding on a name is to support it with an online presence that includes a standout logo, a unified colour scheme, and typography that is consistent across all platforms.

Yes, a lot of thought, hurdles to creativity, and errors are necessary for branding. However, putting your values on display for the public is a worthy exercise.

Chapter Four

Sufficient Promotion

Customers are essential to your business's survival and growth. You must advertise your firm if you want to attract clients. This used to be as simple as selecting between a flyer, brochure, postcard, or local newspaper advertisement.

However, the possibilities in today's digital environment are limitless—that is, overwhelming.

a road map of digital marketing tactics for the most effective company promotion
Image Origin

Thus, you are (a) not alone and (b) in the perfect location if you are having trouble deciding how to market your company or even simply figuring out what your alternatives are.

Whether you have a tight budget, no budget, or some wiggle space, I'll go over the top 30 methods of company promotion in this piece. We will discuss methods to disseminate information about:

search engines (namely, Maps and Google Search).
social networking platforms (such as YouTube, TikTok, Facebook, Instagram, Twitter, LinkedIn, and Pinterest).
Online directory listings: you may be surprised to learn more about them!
Your neighbourhood (press, events, and sponsorships).
If you want to differentiate your company from the competition and attract clients, you must promote it. Let's start with the most widely used platform: Google.

How to advertise your company on Google
It makes perfect sense to advertise your company on Google. With over 90% of the

market, it's among the most effective methods to reach customers who are actively looking for solutions. Here are the top methods for using Google to spread the word about you:

1. Make sure your Google Business Profile is up to date.
Your company can appear in Google Maps results, the local section of Google Search results, and the right-side Knowledge Panel in Search results when someone types in your business name (here are some ideas for creative business names!) and location thanks to your Google Business Profile, which is Google's term for your Google listing. Taking advantage of this free directory listing is highly recommended, especially since Google continues to refine its search results based on the location of the user.

Verifying who owns your listing using your free Google Business account is essential to utilizing your Business Profile to market your company. Once you are the owner, you may make your listing more relevant to searches and appear higher in search results.

greatest strategies to raise your company's position in local search results
Your company is essentially marketing itself around the clock if it appears in the Local Pack (as shown above) of standard search results pages or ranks well on Google Maps. Better still, you may publish articles straight to your Google listing, attracting viewers with eye-catching advertisements at a time when their intent is strongest.

Visit 13 Google My Company Optimizations for a more in-depth look at this very affordable and successful form of company promotion.

2. Obtain a webpage
Any website is an essential component of marketing assets, regardless of how traditional your clientele or company may be. Both existing and new clients visit your website first. They will want to visit your website, which, like your

Google listing, promotes your company 24/7, even if they discover you via social media or Google.

In addition to being a useful marketing tool in and of itself, a well-designed business website is also critical for tracking and enhancing the effectiveness of your other marketing initiatives. It tells the story of your company and what you offer, gives contact details, and embodies the essence of your brand.

A website is among the most effective tools for company promotion.
For instance, landing pages that are hosted on your website are necessary for running advertisements. Your website should be linked to any beneficial content you provide on social media. With data from all of your marketing channels coming into your website, you can utilize analytics to identify the most effective techniques and get an insightful understanding of your target audience.

Even while there are free options for setting up a website for your company, if you want to promote your brand seriously you will almost certainly need to switch to a paid website. Growth requires having your domain name, a polished appearance and feel, and the flexibility to expand and add features as required.

3. Put SEO into practice

It is one thing for you to advertise your company; it is quite another for Google to do the same. A collection of procedures known as SEO helps your company become in line with Google's ranking system. To be more precise and high-quality, search engine optimization is actually about optimizing for searchers, especially those who are specifically looking for what you have to offer since this algorithm has grown to use machine learning and user behaviour.

SEO is a multifaceted strategy that uses a variety of techniques to raise your ranking. Additionally, you have an equal opportunity to appear on

Google's first page—without investing a dime—as major shops do, thanks to the search engine's excellent location-based results! (Of course, excluding the price of obtaining a website).

Best approach to advertise your business: tiny companies showing up in search engine results
Among the SEO strategies to market your company are:

Including location- and industry-specific keywords in certain areas of your website.
generating unique, excellent material regularly and including tagged photos.
keeping security and fast page loads intact.
See our article on The Top 10 Google Ranking Factors of 2020 (+How to Optimize for Them) for further SEO advice.

Google effectively promotes your company for you when it ranks well in search results—and not just to random users, but also to those who are specifically looking for what you have to offer. Better doesn't come much closer than that.

4. Make a blog for your company.

Although we briefly discussed it in the previous plan, content is such a significant SEO driver that it merits its section inside the promotional strategy hierarchy. A blog is not a business's LiveJournal. Sure, you can write a few pieces on accomplishments and events, but the real secret to a successful business blog is to develop informative material in your brand language that revolves around Google searches made by your potential clients.

top strategies for advertising your company blog post

These queries and phrases are known as keywords, and the more material you write with these terms in mind, the more chances your company has to appear on search engine results pages. Any of the above may make for excellent blog posts:

5. Distribute your work

A blog that demonstrates your subject matter knowledge, personability, and sincere desire to assist your readers is an ideal marketing tool for a company. Thus, don't simply post things; encourage them! To assist you in getting leads, you may use social media, email newsletters, or even make them into downloadable manuals. Even better, if you create material with social media sharing in mind, other reputable websites will probably notice your blog posts and link back to your site on their own or in their social media feeds, effectively marketing your brand on your own.

Just keep in mind that it becomes more crucial to ensure that your content loads swiftly the more visitors you get to your website. A content delivery network (CDN) may guarantee speedy content delivery for sizable and/or expanding websites. There are several solutions available; HubSpot, for instance, offers a CDN option.

6. Use Google AdWords

Even if SEO is one of the strongest marketing tactics, it takes time to show effects; it may take weeks or even months. Google Ads is the best option if you have the funds and want greater visibility right now. Above organic and local listings, Google Ads appear at the top of search engine results pages. Furthermore, Google is by far the most widely used search engine out there due to its high degree of flexibility, ad-creating tools, and comprehensive performance analytics, in addition to controlling the majority of search engine traffic.

Google Ads are the finest means of company promotion.

Although it takes some time and a lot of trial and error to become proficient with Google AdWords, the investment in an effective campaign is worth it. Google offers two different ways to advertise: branded banner advertisements on the Display Network and text ads on the Search Network. When you're ready to get going, use our comprehensive guide to run Google AdWords.

If you already run Google Ads, use our Free Google Ads Performance Grader to see how *really* well your campaigns are doing.

How to use Internet directories to market your company
Online directories are often used by customers to find and evaluate companies that meet their unique demands. Because they are often well-established, popular websites with high domain authority, it's normal for your company name or profile page to appear on Google's first page when linked to one of these domains. Making an online listing is quick and easy, and it may improve your online visibility by drawing in local, highly motivated clients.
local listings on the SERP are the finest methods for promoting your company.

7. Make entries in the main directories.
Because smaller directories rely on bigger ones for their data, listing on the main sites will probably also cause you to appear automatically

on lesser directories. A list of the main directories is shown below. While they are all free, several of them offer premium choices for more sophisticated functionality.

8. Make your listings more effective.
Making a listing is one thing; optimizing it is quite another. You may make your company seem better and rank higher in searches by completing all of the fields on your profiles, uploading images, and gathering reviews. Additionally, it's critical to confirm that the data on all of your listings matches the data on your website. If you have inconsistent results, the Goog may become less confident in your credibility. Lastly, keep an eye on your listing and make any necessary corrections—inaccuracies might occur when listings are automatically updated.

9. Obtain online testimonials from clients.
Although we only briefly discussed gathering reviews, they merit their section due to how crucial they are for small and local companies.

One of the most effective ways to get the proper individuals to know about your company is via word-of-mouth marketing. Testimonials from your website are excellent, but official review sites like Yelp, Google, and Facebook have greater ratings.

top strategies for promoting your company on Google Reviews

These websites may help you get more visibility, and consumers trust the evaluations more here than anyplace else since they take precautions against spam and fraudulent reviews. Furthermore, a significant ranking element for local search results is reviews. To get reviews, see these posts:

How to Request Evaluations (with Samples)

These 16 Tried and True Strategies Will Help You Get More Google Reviews

10. Keep an eye on and reply to reviews

Since anybody may add a listing to many internet directories, your company can still be there and accumulate ratings even if you didn't list it. When at all feasible, be sure to claim your listings, and keep a close eye on these websites. You may reply to evaluations in this manner, which is an additional excellent method of advertising your company. You may not only address (and even reverse) unfavourable evaluations, but you can also communicate your brand's values to prospective clients by responding to both good and bad reviews.

How to use social media to advertise your company

Another cost-free method of spreading the word about your small company is social networking. While Facebook, Instagram, LinkedIn, and Twitter are the most often used platforms for business accounts, don't forget to use other websites that may be relevant to your industry, such as Reddit or Pinterest.

11. Give Facebook priority.

Being the biggest social network on the internet, Facebook may be a terrific tool for connecting with current clients and attracting new ones. Depending on your sector, Facebook company promotion may take many different forms, but here are some fundamentals:

Make a Facebook business page with a call to action and your contact details.
To increase attendance and promote your events, use Facebook events.
Organize Facebook live events with instructional or exclusive behind-the-scenes looks.
Facebook Live is the finest method to advertise your company, whether you have money or not.
See our article, 22 Facebook Marketing Tips for Small Businesses on a Budget, for other ideas on how to use Facebook to market your company.

Additionally, remember Facebook advertisements!

Facebook advertising enables you to target users based on a wide range of personal information, including hobbies, employment, marital status, and more. This lets you reach very targeted audiences. See our article on The 8 Best (and Free!) Facebook Ads Courses for Any Level for more information on how to start or even enhance your Facebook advertising.

Make sure you're not wasting money on Facebook advertising if you're currently doing it by using our Free Facebook Ads Performance Grader!

12. Join and contribute to LinkedIn.
LinkedIn has evolved into more than simply a place to upload your CV; you can now use it for general online networking, group conversations, connecting with prospective clients, and forming new relationships. Before conducting business with you, potential clients might look you or your firm up to learn more about you and your staff's backgrounds and number of workers.

By offering your opinions in group conversations and/or by including links to pertinent material on your website, you may further indirectly market your company on

LinkedIn. Just watch out that you don't constantly advertise your work.

13. Place videos on YouTube.

You may advertise your company effectively using videos on YouTube for free! Using YouTube to promote your company is a great method to build a relationship with prospective clients or consumers. You may use a short film that you made as a sales tool to send out emails to potential customers or to display on the homepage of your website. Simply put together and publish the movie on YouTube.

To attract customers searching for what your company provides, you may also upload instructional films, guides, or how-tos to your YouTube channel. Check out our page on DIY at-home films to see some of the many reasonably priced choices available for creating videos. Additionally, you may use videos in your blog articles to improve their SEO quality. An example of this is the WordStream post below:

top strategies for company promotion: include a YouTube video in your blog post

Also take note of the fact that videos often appear at the top of search results for really specialized queries, such as this one:

top strategies for marketing your company how-to videos

14. Promote your channel on YouTube.

If done correctly, YouTube advertising has the potential to provide financial returns, just like the other paid techniques discussed in this essay. YouTube allows you to promote via text advertisements that show up in search results or by making video ads that play before videos in related categories:

The finest techniques to advertise on YouTube and promote your company

15. Use Instagram to interact with your followers.

Instagram is the third most popular social networking site, despite being one of the more recent ones to be introduced. Instagram has a multitude of publishing types, including live sessions, story highlights, IGTV series, permanent photos, and more, so you can utilize it in several ways to interact with your audience and market your brand. One may:

Use hashtags to spread the word about your specials and sales to a wider audience.

Organize competitions offering free or heavily discounted goods or services to create goodwill (and to get a list of potential customers to contact).

To become recognized as a trusted q, provide guidance and lessons.

See these 11 Instagram marketing strategies for further ideas on how to use Instagram to promote your brand.

16. Put on Twitter

Another free platform for Internet company promotion is Twitter, which you should utilize if the majority of your target audience is between the ages of 18 and 24. Building a following usually takes a little more work, but if you're on

the site often, you may become an expert user and reap its rewards.
the ideal method to advertise your company on Twitter by requesting clients to visit

17. Try Pinterest out.

Even though the core purpose of Pinterest is picture sharing, the ability for your photographs to connect back to your website is a chance to advertise your company and increase website traffic.

Because Pinterest users are mostly female, it is particularly effective for e-commerce companies trying to attract a female audience. If this describes you, you may want to consider being involved in the Pinterest network.

18. Check out TikTok

Despite just being created in 2016, TikTok now has more active users than Twitter, LinkedIn, Snapchat, Pinterest, and others. It's a fantastic video marketing tool that's not only for millennials because of how simple it is to create eye-catching videos with special effects. You may use the platform immediately to post instructional, how-to, and behind-the-scenes videos, but you might also want to use the example below to spread the word about your newly created TikTok channel on other social media platforms:

top strategies for company promotion—a Tiktok video posted on Facebook

19. Participate in internet forums

Putting a helping hand up for others is one of the finest methods to go ahead. Become a member of networks and groups on LinkedIn, Reddit, and Facebook that are related to your company or sector. When individuals ask questions or have difficulties, give them sound advice. (Of course, make sure the information on your profile links back to your company.)

LinkedIn groups and other online communities are excellent means of promoting your company.

Building a real reputation and strong relationships with individuals who are important to your job may be achieved in this manner. In general, one gets what goes around. And never forget that a thousand quiet people are watching you, seeing your name and what you're doing, even while you assist one person with their question.

20. Consider working together on influencer marketing.

Influencers are well-known figures in your field, and your company may participate in both geographically and specialized-based groups. They may not be presenting talk programs or walking the red carpet, but they are immensely well-liked, very trustworthy, and well-respected authorities in your field. Influencers have a sizable social media and/or blog following, so having your company acknowledged or highlighted by one of them may expose it to a wide, relevant audience.

Still, influencer marketing is a very cautious tactic. Before contacting an influencer, spend some time getting to know their accounts on all social media platforms; leave comments on, like, and share their material; and make sure you approach them with a clear request and something of comparable value in return. For instance, you might give them a free month of sessions in return for a blog review and social media mentions. Alternatively, you might offer to provide a well-written guest article that links back to your website and helps their readership on their blog.

21. Spend money on social media marketing

One of the most inventive, popular, and successful types of digital advertising available today is social media advertising. It is used by over 3.6 BILLION people and is always changing to provide great value for your advertising spend along with simplicity of use. When used correctly, sponsored social media marketing offers the following benefits to a highly focused audience for your business:

Get to know individuals by using the channels they often use.

Cost-effectiveness: With advanced targeting, you can be confident that only the most appropriate audience sees your adverts.

Supporting material: Your sponsored posts are bolstered by the content from your organic posts.

Brand loyalty: Growing your following on social media platforms fosters a sense of community and brand loyalty for your company.

Analytics: Determine what is effective so that you may allocate funds appropriately.

How to advertise your company in the neighborhood

The community plays a vital role in the development of local enterprises. Naturally, retailers and restaurants are aware of this implicitly, and even companies with a larger global emphasis nonetheless feel a strong connection to the location or locations in which they do business. Having stated that, let's discuss a few strategies for local small-company marketing.

22. Aim for local media attention

Pitching your company's activities to the local press might be frightening for some reason, yet local blogs, newspapers, and online publications are constantly looking for new material.

See if you can write an article for your local news outlets, whether it's a thought-provoking essay, a resource list, or a noteworthy update about your company. You may even be able to persuade someone else to publish a featured article if the narrative of your company is interesting enough.

top strategies for promoting your company in local media

You may also offer a local writer to come for free in return for a recap, or you can ask them to write about an event you are throwing in your neighbourhood.

If you can afford it, you can even think about working with a public relations agency, app, or partner to have your tales picked up by other media outlets. You may publish your press releases using websites like www.prweb.com if you have a somewhat less budget. By including links back to your website, these press releases may aid in search engine optimization and perhaps get picked up by media sources.

23. Create alliances

Promoting your company in your local network may be accomplished by forming partnerships with companies that cater to the same audience but aren't competitors. After you have a partnership established, you may use your email lists, in-store flyers or discounts, and social media engagement to cross-promote each other's services. To get the most out of the partnership's promotional potential, don't be hesitant to use your imagination.

24. Interaction

Increasing your visibility in your town may be achieved by participating in local networking activities. Certain companies are more suited for this than others. Local networking will be significantly more fruitful if you provide services directly to customers or other small companies rather than, say, selling things online. All networking, however, is beneficial, even if it's merely to exchange ideas and motivation with other entrepreneurs.

These low-cost marketing strategies may bring in a plethora of new clients and consumers for your organization, both online and off.

And if you do engage in networking—I'm not here to dictate how you should live your life—be sure to take advantage of my nine templates for networking emails, which include the one below: top strategies for company promotion: networking email

25. Participate in, organize, or fund local activities

Even in this increasingly digital age, supporting, organizing, or attending local events is a terrific way to advertise your company and build relationships with the people who use it.

You may volunteer to teach at a local school, library, or other business, conduct a lesson at your place, or just throw a fun, family-friendly event during a particular season. Make the most of the time you invested in designing and instructing the class by having a buddy record you in action and posting the result on YouTube and your website.

26. Try sending a straight letter.

Even with the prevalence of digital media these days, direct mail campaigns including postcards, flyers, letters, and other materials may still be very successful in drawing in local clients. The inability to precisely target your mailings is one of the main drawbacks of this advertising strategy; thus, to get a response, you will need to print up and send out a large amount of mail. The advantage is that, with proper execution, direct mail marketing may help you attract new clients via a very scalable method.

direct mail is the finest method for company promotion.

To keep your devoted clients coming back and (probably) encouraging them to tell their friends and family about your company, you might also offer them little gift packages around the holidays.

27. Both offline and local advertising
Traditional media outlets such as newspapers, magazines, radio, and television are also good options for advertising your company. If you're thinking about using print advertisements or any of these offline marketing techniques to promote your company, the most important thing is to make sure you're monitoring everything so you can determine how successful it is.

Other successful company promotion strategies
Considering how I arranged the ideas in this essay, these three promotional tactics are the last but most certainly not the least.

28. Go to trade exhibits
Attending a large trade show might make sense if you want to market your items to shops and

are aiming for a national audience. whether you aren't sure whether attending the trade show would benefit you and you have time to make up your mind, you may want to consider going as a guest instead of spending the money for a booth. A firm you have a solid working connection with that is already scheduled to present at a trade show can allow you to "hang out" at their booth for a while so you can watch and learn, and you might even get free advertising for your business.

29. Conduct email marketing initiatives.
Despite the long history of email marketing, the tactic has not lost its effectiveness. Compared to other forms of communication, 77% of respondents would rather receive permission-based promotional communications via email. Email is a widely used medium by both companies and consumers:

People like being knowledgeable.
People check their email all the time.
Email provides thorough reporting.

To send out customized, targeted emails, you may segment your lists.

There is an average 30x return on investment from email marketing.

Platforms for email marketing provide adaptability, inventiveness, and—above all—user-friendliness.

email marketing is one of the finest strategies to advertise your company.

See How to Write Undelete-able Promotional Emails, one of my posts, for further advice on email marketing.

30. Turn your staff members become evangelists
When you treat your staff well and exercise good leadership, they will become natural brand ambassadors for your company. Organize brainstorming sessions, reward blog post submissions from staff members, have fireside talks, engage them in neighbourhood activities, and organize family and friend promotions. If you appreciate your employees, they will value the company they work for. After that, you may promote social media sharing and provide them

with news and resources so they can easily tell others about your company.

Chapter Five

Distinctive Client Support

What elements are crucial to provide top-notch customer service? This is a question you should be asking yourself if you operate a company. Your bottom line is directly impacted by customer happiness, so knowing what matters most to your consumers can help you retain them as well as grow sales. Business success is significantly influenced by customer happiness.

The top things that I've discovered clients cherish most when they get exceptional customer service are listed below. Make sure to take into account the following elements to make sure your clients feel appreciated and get what they want from their interaction with you (and without any hassle):

1. Show consideration for your clients.

Consumers like to feel important and respected. They don't want to be minimized or disregarded. Make sure you act with respect and in a friendly, pleasant manner while assisting customers.

2. Offer timely support.

Customers, in my experience, detest having to wait. They often don't want to wait around for assistance and want it immediately. Install a system that enables clients to get help promptly. This might include having a phone agent on duty or customer service agents on hand who can handle complaints from clients quickly.

3. Locate solutions that satisfy the demands of the client.

Many clients detest dealing with the same problem over and over again in addition to having to wait. They want answers that address their particular requirements and concerns.

When offering customer support, spend time getting to know the client's needs and coming up with a solution that suits them. Make sure that any issues are handled effectively and as soon as possible to avoid making the consumer return.

4. Communicate succinctly and plainly.
Make sure clients understand what is going on and what they need to do. When offering customer support, ensure sure all of your messages are understandable and unambiguous. This entails speaking plainly and staying away from jargon.

5. When anything goes wrong, be sincere.
Honesty is valued by customers. When anything goes wrong, people usually expect firms to be honest about it and find out what went wrong. Always be truthful with customers and don't attempt to conceal anything when you encounter problems.

6. Prioritize client happiness and a feeling of concern.
Customers, it seems to me, want to believe that they are the only ones who count and that

companies care about them. Make sure you are keeping the demands of that particular consumer in mind and are taking all reasonable steps to meet their needs. Make the additional effort to assist the consumer to demonstrate your concern for their experience.

7. Keep a cheerful outlook.

Most of us can likely tell when someone is dissatisfied or unwilling to assist us; avoid allowing this to occur in your customer service. It's critical to have a positive outlook and demonstrate your excitement to assist the client. They may feel more valued and welcomed as a result.

8. Inform the people on your team about your company.

The majority of individuals prefer to collaborate with experts in their field. Make certain that the employees are informed on the goods and services you provide. Additionally, this will enable them to promptly and successfully handle client complaints.

These are just a few of the most important elements of first-rate customer service. Make sure you concentrate on these crucial areas if you want to maintain your consumers' happiness and satisfaction. As there are a lot of details to manage when managing a company, try to make the customer experience as easy and enjoyable as you can for your customers.

Chapter Six

Keeping Your Clientele.

During this Thanksgiving week, are you feeling grateful for your team, or are you worried that one of your key players may step down?

When you take into account the cost of recruiting, training, and lost productivity, replacing a lost team member usually costs 150 per cent of the employee's compensation. So, give these three quick examples some thought and see how you might keep your top employees on board throughout the year.

1. Do, hear, and ask.
When workers feel appreciated and heard, they remain on the job. Last month, I spoke with a disgruntled valet at a high-end hotel who was rushing back and forth from the parking lot to the hotel's entrance. He informed me that they could deliver automobiles 50% quicker if they had a radio to speak with the other members of

the valet service since visitors would often leave missing goods in their cars. No one had paid attention to his suggestion. You cease voicing your opinions when you've been rejected twice. How are you hearing what your team has to say and acting upon it?

2. Honor devoted staff members

At the Laguna Cliffs Marriott hotel, our waitress had a name tag with her 25-year service history on it. When I inquired, she gladly shared with me several anecdotes about her and her coworkers who had been there since the hotel's founding. She also mentioned how the hotel had accommodated her request for fewer hours when she had young children, allowing her to work in the restaurant, which was her favourite job. Even though many people may only have fond memories of receiving gold watch retirement presents from a single employer, recognize and honour your long-serving staff members by making it a point of your customer service differentiation.

3. Get immediate feedback from customers.

Towards the conclusion of my summer journey with Air New Zealand, a crew member approached me and asked how I felt about my cabin host, Vera. I gave her the examples and tales she requested. They only asked me for my tales; there were no checkboxes or long questionnaires. After the trip, Air New Zealand shares these anecdotes with the crew right away since it cheers up flight attendants to hear firsthand accounts and comments from the clients they just served. It is significantly more meaningful to hear someone's narrative than to find out that you are 67% happy. How can you get genuine, impactful, and emotional client feedback and distribute it to your staff?

4. Never fall into the Talent Fallacy.

Think of your team as including three groups: the high performers, the low performers, and the rest of the group. Who occupies the most of your time and effort? Many leaders unwittingly find themselves spending most of their time with people who are underperforming or who are not a good fit for their present role and expectations, which has decreasing rewards. The idea that your best employees need less of your time and attention is false. You will get much more out of your work if you consciously decide to give your best-performing team members priority on your schedule today.

You may be surprised to learn how much more power you have over keeping your finest individuals around. Since immediate managers are the main cause of employee resignations, try one of these suggestions and think about what more you can do right now to ensure that all of the managers in your organization are managing.